Summer / December 2013
The Faery Issue
www.inspiritmagazine.com

Editor's Note

Phew! What a relief and breath of fresh air the energy of this issue feels like, after the heaviness and challenge of 2013.

This issue brings the lightness, fun and enjoyment of the Faery as they flutter their wings spreading magical Faery dust over all of you. For me, this is bringing a lightening of my heart and a clearer focus on the directions going forward into 2014. I pray that this is true for you too and with it comes great abundance from all the hard work and effort you put in.

To bring some of the Faery magic to this issue we couldn't go pass the sensational work of the Froud family. Known for creating other worldly magic in such films as the Labyrinth and the Dark Crystal, Brian and Wendy Froud have so much to share when it comes to the elemental world. We are grateful that they could find some time to work with Nicola.

Each of us have brought together our own expression of the Faery and inSpired wisdoms, so I'm sure you'll enjoy a variety of perspectives on this unique topic. Perhaps you will even find one that speaks to you, just as I did with Serene Conneeley's article "Faeries as a personification of nature" and its unique approach to this topic.

With this issue we introduce a small fee to access inSpirit Magazine online. There is a lot of time, energy and effort that goes into creating inSpirit each quarter along with the fact that it is time for the magazine to financially sustain itself. Your small contribution of $1.99 will go along way to giving back to our contributors and ensuring a long life for inSpirit Magazine. This also provides us the perfect opportunity to introduce a monthly newsletter. inSpirit has been growing in content, and with the intention of the bridging the gap with it's frequency we believe our monthly newsletter will add even more valuable educational and informative information, which inSpirit is known for.

Lastly, this is the last issue that the lovely Julia Inglis of Sacred Familiar will contribute. Julia's Swan Blessing Past Life stories have been a valuable and unique addition to inSpirit magazine. Julia is venturing forth in new directions with a lot of gratitude from myself, the inSpirit team and community. We wish her and her partner Tony all the very best with their future endeavours. Thank you Julia and Tony for your connection, contributions and loving energy.

With love & gratitude, Kerrie

THE TEAM

CREATIVE TEAM Kerrie Wearing, Nicolle Poll, Nicola McIntosh, Alex Cayas
EDITOR Nicolle Poll
MANAGING EDITOR Kerrie Wearing
REGULAR CONTRIBUTORS Kerrie Wearing, Nicolle Poll, Nicola McIntosh, Susanne Hartas, Billie Dean, Julia Inglis, Brendan D. Murphy, Gem~mer, Meadow Linn, Alex Cayas, Natasha Heard, Laura Naomi, Kye Crow, Reilly McCarron, Rita Maher
GUEST CONTRIBUTORS Brian & Wendy Froud, David Wells, Serene Conneeley, Lee Spinks
GRAPHIC DESIGN Nicola McIntosh
COVER ARTWORK Brian Froud

Produced by Kerrie Wearing and inSpirit Publishing, inSpirit Magazine is designed to provide a respectful forum for like-minded souls to share in a community which aims to provide informative views, opinions and education regarding the experience of living with Spirit. Disclaimer: While every care has been taken to provide the reader with accurate, inSpiring and thought-provoking information, the Publishers take no responsibility for the accuracy of information and views expressed by the Contributors. The views and opinions expressed by contributors are not necessarily shared by the Editor Publishers.

In This Issue

6   Brian & Wendy Froud: Faeries' Tales

3	Faery Beginnings
4	Year Ahead 2014
8	Faery as a Personification of Nature
10	Lunar New Year - The Year of the Wood Horse
11	The Magic of Sacred Stones
12	Wisdom from the Fae
14	Faery Flashback
15	Clothing from the Faery Realm
16	Faery Messages
18	Magical Realms
19	The Swan Blessing - Never Lift the Veil
21	Faery Files: Case Pending
22	Fairies, Gods, Aliens and Jesters - Abtruse Connections
24	Muddy Hands and Feet
25	Spirit Meals Welcome Magic

Regular Columns

17	Goddess inSpiration
20	For the Love of Angels
26	inSpirit Reviews
27	inSpirit Directory

19

15

16

12

Faery Beginnings

by Lee Spinks

It was going back fourteen years ago when my family and I moved into an old country house. The paddocks were studded with huge Gum trees and sheep roamed around baaing. There was not another house in sight, peace and serenity flowed with the waving of the long dry grass in the breeze.

The house took a lot of cleaning and fixing, but after a few years it was looking great. I put in a chook house and a vegetable garden and all of the gardens and trees were flourishing. I would put the Golden Orb spider's that lived there in my vege garden and they would make their webs around the tomatoes and keep the fruit fly out of them. It was a magical place; it was there when I got my soul cat 'Merlin', who is curled up on my lap asleep at this very moment.

In 2003 I was settled, happy and content. My spiritual side was out in full bloom, my intuition was high and it was the most I'd ever been in contact with the other side.

One spring afternoon I was having a snooze on the lounge when I had the most amazing awakening, as I opened my eyes I could see a little orb about an inch or more in size floating slowly just above the floor. I closed my eyes and re-opened them. *'Am I seeing things?'* I thought. It was still there glowing a golden lime. I sat up and rubbed my eyes and looked again, it was still there moving towards the other lounge. So I just sat there stunned watching it disappear under the lounge, I shook my head and got up and did more chores around the house.

That night I went to bed and did my nightly chakra balancing, always asking for protection I opened my crowning lotus chakra and brought down the white light, spiraling slowly down into my body and touching all of my chakra's making them glow big and bright. Then the green light for healing, the pink for unconditional love and last one, purple to help heighten my spiritual vibrations. But then to my surprise in came the most shiniest silvery light, radiating sparkles. *'WOW! This is truly something special, what is this'* I asked? Then at the same time of my question a beautiful lady floated down towards me, her face was white and translucent and her hair long and swirling around. As she got closer she looked at me with the most pleasing look, I could now see her eyebrows swirling as well, above her blue green eyes. I could feel her like she was a part of me and then she said, "For the silver light the world awaits!" Then she slowly descended back up as she said "I am the Faery Queen".

I was entranced by this sensational moment and then something clicked *'Oh God! I have to draw her before I forget what she looks like'* and jumped quickly out of bed. This is the original drawing, I have kept it in my art draw and have tried to paint her but I have never been able to capture the true her.

Since then I can see faeries, little tiny silver sparks that dart around in front or beside me. First I could see them in the garden and then inside, along with frogs and lizard, having many experiences with them.

But the most spectacular time was a year later when my brother died, I awoke the next morning to find thousands of faeries in my room hovering above me sending me their condolences and letting me know that they are here for me. The loss of my brother compelled me to write as a way to get my grieving out, I wrote a poem called *Eternal Life*.

After that the Faerie Queen came back to me. After a year of thinking about exactly what she meant about the silver light, she spoke the words "Then the golden dawn will break". My poetry flowed out of me like it was coming from another realm and are about saving our world and how nature is our sacred temple. We need to appreciate how fortunate we are to be living on this rare jewel in the universe. We are the silver light that the world awaits for and we need to do as much as we can to preserve it and regenerate it for the future. The Golden Dawn!

Year Ahead 2014

INTRODUCTION - This year sees very little movement from the larger outer planets but a continuation of the confrontation between Pluto and Uranus makes for even more strides towards a more independent, free thinking economy through individual questioning of what's true and what's good marketing from those in power. On a personal level this is likely to make you question everything from government to your boss, just what is the real agenda? Mars in Libra for an extraordinary seven months pushes relationship buttons; there can be no harmony without conflict. Jupiter is in fabulous Leo from the middle of the year, dramas are par for the course but what course, set your soul's satnav toward freedom of expression.

Aries
21st Mar – 20th Apr

Bumpy isn't necessarily a bad thing, bumpy means you can go where others fear to tread and bumpy means you learn to deal with roads less travelled. This year you're making it clear that you are looking for a new kind of normal and as you rock your way out of rut you will upset some folks but maintaining your own integrity sometimes means that has to happen. You're naturally independent Aries but don't see that as having to go it alone, Mars will be in your opposite sign for the first half of the year and he wants you to find someone perfect, perfectly capable of dealing with your more heated moments and from July that baton is handed over to Jupiter who helps true love happen. Nice.

Gemini
21st May – 20th June

From the off you may be encouraging someone to get to know you better, that's just fine but make sure you know where the boundaries lie or maybe what you want them to know? Keeping secrets won't be easy this year Gemini so maybe it's best not to have any, and personal relationships certainly flow better when you are open and honest. For single Gemini this year works very well and flirting is your national sport with medals being awarded in the early months, but to truly win you may want to secure something longer term before Mars and his flirt-o-meter run out in May. You're very wordy, more so than usual, this year so write that book, send in a screenplay or take acting lessons; like you need them?

Leo
23rd July – 22nd Aug

Yes, lucky Jupiter is in your sign from the 16th of July and no doubt you've already spent the windfall he can bring but hang on Leo. Even though he will then spend a whole year with you he will move in reverse, challenge other planets and be challenged in return so maybe you could embrace the idea that opportunity doesn't always come with ribbon and bows? Sometimes it's tough choices and harsh conversations that create openings and that may be the case earlier in the year, clearing away the debris to make Jupiter's transit easier for you? Dramas there will be, some may not even be created by you, but most will, it's what you do to move things along. And what of love? Meh. Not so busy.

Taurus
21st Apr – 20th May

You work hard and no matter what anyone says you know that you will be rewarded for that without making any sudden moves, without taking your talents elsewhere and without the need to create any dramas like the rest of the world. Really? It all depends on how far you want to go this year Taurus? Your working life is a very strong focus and the world is your oyster, if you want to travel then send out your CV and see what invitations come back. Knowing your subject could see you sign up for a course, offered extra training or encouraged to teach which is in itself a form or learning of course. Love is steady, someone who is prepared to wait does indeed wait!

Cancer
21st June – 22nd July

You will lose the benefits of Jupiter in your sign from July 16th this year and it will be twelve years before he returns, so get to filling in those immigration forms, sort out your overseas travel, sign up for Uni or make your feelings known to your local nunnery, get a jigsaw and a simple brown suitcase and join in. Faith, travel, education and a good old knees up with the rest of the sisters is in order. From the July 16th thoughts turn to worldly goods as Jupiter put cash in your pockets and as your day to day work ruler it's likely to come through promotion where you are now. Other avenues are possible with those overseas connections stronger than ever. As for love; it's like last year, highs and lows, lows and highs and singles have a high that isn't as low as last year. Win win.

Virgo
23rd Aug – 22nd Sept

When you have itchy feet you either scratch them or you sit and get agitated, which one is to be? Your start the year with ideas of how things could be different, ideas put into your head by those who have got up and got on with things, but pretty soon things change and there's comfort in routine, settling for being in the same place with the same people and as the exciting ones move on you may stay where you are. But as June and July move in you get restless again as talk turns towards seeking dream jobs, dream loves or dreams come true. Get a plan, stick to it and no matter how awkward a family member or boss gets know that ultimately your fate is in your hands. Scratch it.

Libra
23rd Sept – 22nd Oct

So you got a mention in the introduction and that means you've got to be up there with the signs most likely to . . . ? To do what exactly Libra? To wear yourself out trying to do too much all at once, to be slightly angst ridden in love or to shout rather than simply talk things through; it's Mars who's in your sign not Tinkerbelle. This isn't a bad thing, it's very far from it, in fact it's one of the most amazing starts to a year for a very long time but you must be ready to stand by you, stand by the real you and to shout to be heard if you have to. With money, love, work and family it's your time to lead so get your head on and get out there and make some changes Magic.

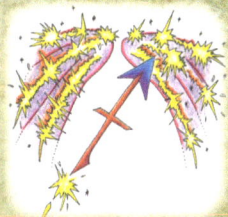
Sagittarius
22nd Nov – 21st Dec

Mates are great aren't they? They do stuff without asking for anything in return and when they need a favour you're first in line to help them out, that's how it goes. This year however Sagittarius things go extreme on you, things go from favour to life changing events and be that you helping them or they helping you don't be shy at taking up any offers. The grand cross, a big X marks the spot in your chart, in April and December offer you a change that may be challenging but if you're up for it you can profit both financially and emotionally. Courage is a given, adventure is your thing but just how far are you prepared to extend yourself to make dreams come true? Life without limits, your new motto.

Aquarius
20th Jan– 18th Feb

As you seek to embrace a world of difference in 2014 you may start off gathering funds, making money to make other things possible and you can do that better than most when you focus, so focus! You're making some new contacts that could help you set up your own business, seek employment abroad or help you gain the necessary experience to get noticed. Love is blossoming in the latter part of the year with someone who you've already had a connection with but never quite got as up close and personal as you would have liked or it's an opportunity to renew vows or settle into a long distance love match that could actually work. Spontaneity is where it's at for your Aquarius, as always, just make sure you don't burn any bridges you may need to cross again.

Scorpio
23rd Oct– 21st Nov

Saturn continues in your sign for another year, he does dip out in late December for a few months then back in 2015 before finally leaving, so it does mean you're still on the list of signs going through major changes. The thing is he's in his last trimester, so that means he really does want to see tangible evidence of change after a couple of years where you've let go of the old and replaced it with shiny new. From the middle of the year Jupiter begins a repair program that puts you ahead with any professional choices and those who may have temporarily stepped over you provide a nice set of shoulders for you stand on as you climb higher still. One word of warning, do it; don't just dream about doing it!

Capricorn
22nd Dec – 19th Jan

The presence of Pluto in your sign is demanding, tougher on those born in the middle of Capricorn's rule this year, but he's a planet that transforms as in caterpillar to butterfly, phoenix through flames or sheds his skin to make way for the new. Painful? Not necessarily Capricorn, they all take the time they are allotted, no more, no less. Give into that process this year, do not try to force anything and all will be well. Your professional life is a priority in the first half, stay true to those who have supported you in the past and your rewards will come. After July relationships get much easier but investments and bigger sums of money need more attention. Transform.

Pisces
19th Feb – 20th Mar

Neptune in your sign makes you more ethereal than ever and whilst that can be a very endearing quality it can also make sure that nobody sees you at all. It's a fine line between appearing otherworldly and disappearing from this one. Jupiter is encouraging new friendships early in the year, new romance if you're looking for that, and as he does your social scene expands meaning less of the staying in and way more of the going out in 2014. Good. You're preparing for a very busy time on the work front and you do that by making sure you accept challenges and opportunities now. What you learn now will make you the expert everyone will be seeking when your once every thirty-year high for work comes round in 2015.

With successful television appearances on programmes such as Your Stars, Jane Goldman Investigates, Big Brother, Fame Academy, RI:SE, GMTV, Heaven on Earth and Most Haunted, David Wells is a popular household name within the paranormal genre. He is an outstanding astrologer, past life therapist, author, teacher and presenter whose unique sense of humour and vibrant personality captivates audiences far and wide. To contact David please visit his website at www.davidwells.co.uk

Artwork Credit – 'Zodiac Faery Wings' Series by Nicolle Poll ● www.facebook.com/ArtworkByNicolle

Faeries' Tales

Creative pioneers Brian and Wendy Froud share with Nicola McIntosh insights about their latest book "Faeries' Tales" and what it is truly like living in the magickal World of Froud…

Nicola: How did you come to do this work, did it choose you? Do you find that sometimes you both create the same character at the same time because you pick up on the energy of whomever is trying to show themselves?

Brian: Actually, I believe that this particular book DID choose me. I began painting large portraits of faeries about two years ago. The faeries seemed to want to be "up close and personal" - not distant, but portrayed as just faces looking directly at the viewer. I began a whole series of these paintings, each one seeming to urgently need to come forward and express something important. I ended up with a group of about forty paintings, each one quite confrontational in some ways - at least in so much as they demand a direct connection with the viewer. I was thinking of putting them together by themselves in a book the I would have called "The Face of Faerie", but our publisher asked us to do another large book along the same lines as "Trolls" which was published last year, and so Wendy and I decided to combine these large portraits with writing as well as sketches and 3D work. We came up with "Faeries' Tales" - a book that lets the faeries tell their own versions of tales we humans are already familiar with, while letting us see and "know" the faery telling the tale. It ended up being quite an intimate book with the viewer and reader meeting each faery as an individual.

Wendy: It was an amazing experience to write for this book. Each portrait - each faery had so much to say. As soon as I really looked at the face in front of me, I began to know what the story was - what that particular faery was telling me. Sometimes it was quite surprising and not at all what I had imagined I would write. Some of them were very funny, but many of them were serious – poignant and rather melancholy. They almost all highlighted our relationship with Faerie but let us see it from their point of view. It felt like they had SO much to say and had just been waiting for Brian to paint them into existence so I could hear what they wanted to tell us. We also have a story running through the book (rather like Trolls) where we follow the adventures of a small faery family called "The Dusters". This will appeal to children and we can imagine parents reading the story to them as they explore the book as a whole. We do talk a bit about how this all came together in our introductions in the book itself.

Nicola: Why do you feel that faeries do or cannot show themselves fully to everyone and how does your work weave itself through your everyday spirituality?

Wendy & Brian: It's very rare for faeries to show themselves physically to humans - even those who are attuned to the energy of Faerie. We see them mostly in our "minds' eye". They DO appear fully formed in our minds. But - one of the most important things to remember about communicating with Faeries or individual faeries is to PAY ATTENTION! We humans walk through our world with no awareness of what is going on around us. Brian and I feel that faeries are right there with us just waiting to be acknowledged - leaving signs of their presence along our path. A stone that stands out in some way, a twig or leaf that gets our attention, a bird's egg or just the way the sun comes through the trees sometimes – these are all reminders (I speak only for Brian and myself) of not only the visible world around us, but the unseen world that exists along side us - the Faerie Realm. Once we are "aware", we can listen to what they have to tell us as well. It's an interesting, on-going relationship that needs to be continually worked at and worked with.

Nicola: Is there a message that the faeries want us to hear by coming through your work?

Wendy & Brian: I think perhaps the message that we (Brian and I) feel the faeries are trying to get across to us is, again - be aware, pay attention and live on this earth knowing that you aren't the only important thing here. We have never gotten direct messages about specific and especially environmental things but we feel that when you are more "in touch" with the Faerie realm you truly become more concerned with the environment and do what ever you can to not damage it. "Treading lightly" becomes more important somehow. Sometimes it seems that the faeries are just bemused by what we humans do or don't do. They don't expect much from us so when we acknowledge them and actually ask for their help, they can be quite delighted to help us - sometimes even over enthusiastic (it's important to really think about what you're asking for)!

Nicola: What's coming up for you in 2014? When will your new book be released and where will we be able to get it from?

Brian & Wendy: We are going to try to teach a bit more in 2014. We will both be teaching and lecturing at the Illustration Master Classes in Amherst, Massachusetts this June. We will also be holding small workshops in our house. We'll have all of that information up on our website and facebook page when we get it sorted out! "Brian Froud's Faeries' Tales" will be released in September/October and should be available everywhere - on Amazon and hopefully in local bookshops in Australia as well as the U.S. and U.K. We will also have an exhibition in New York at the AFA gallery in conjunction with the book release.

Nicola: Are you discovering new things the deeper you get into Faery?

Brian: I'm not sure I'm discovering "new" things as much as uncovering old things and exploring different aspects of things I already know. I've been on the Faery Path for many years now. It's a path I can't step off of. I've dedicated my life and my art to Faerie and this is where I'm bound to stay!

Nicola: Do you have any long-term goals that you wish to complete?

Brian & Wendy: Not sure about long-term goals. We do what we do and hope that it resonates with those who come in contact with it and with us. Probably a long-term goal is to just be able to continue doing what we do. People assume that because we are well known, we have an easy life. It isn't easy at all - it's rewarding and it's a vocation - but it isn't easy!

Brian Froud was born in Winchester, England in 1947. He grew up in Kent and graduated with a first class honors degree from Maidstone College of Art.

He began his career by illustrating book covers and quickly went on to illustrating many books including "The Land Of Froud', The award winning "Faeries" with Alan Lee and more recently "Lady Cottington's Pressed Faery Book" and "Good Faeries, Bad Faeries".

Brian also designed the award winning and cult films "The Dark Crystal" and "Labyrinth" for Jim Henson.

Brian's most recent books are "The Faery Oracle" with Jessica Macbeth and "Lady Cottington's Faery Album", the republished classic "The World of The Dark Crystal", "The Runes Of Elfland" and "Goblins! " with author, Ari Berk, "Brian Froud's Secret sketchbook", "Lady Cottington's Pressed Faery Letters" with Ari Berk , "Brian Froud's World of Faerie" , " The Heart of Faerie Oracle" with Wendy Froud and recently published "How To See Faeries" with John Matthews and "Trolls" with Wendy Froud in 2012.

Brian has exhibited in museums and galleries throughout the U.S, U.K. , Europe and Japan and his work is represented in private collections throughout the world. He is an

Academician of The British SouthWest Academy of Fine and Applied Arts.

Brian has been the recipient of many awards including the Hugo award, Chesley and Inkpot as well as the American Society of Illustrators.

Wendy Froud was born in Detroit, Michigan in 1954. She graduated with a BFA in Fine Art (concentrating on fabric design and ceramics) from The Center For Creative Studies College of Art and Design in Detroit.

Wendy moved to New York where after receiving one of her puppets as a Christmas gift from the Muppet's art director, Jim Henson asked her to come and work on their newest project, "The Dark Crystal" where she met her husband to be, Brian Froud. Wendy worked not only on The Dark Crystal but on the Muppet Show, Muppet Movie, The Empire Strikes Back (as fabricator of Yoda) and Labyrinth.

Since moving permanently to Dartmoor, England, Wendy has concentrated on making models and mythic figures. She has illustrated three books - "A Midsummer Night's Faerytale", "The Winter Child", and "The Faeries of Spring Cottage" - with author Terri Windling.

Imaginosis published a book of Wendy's writings illustrated with her dolls and figures -The Art of Wendy Froud. She also writes for magazines and has had her fiction writing included in two anthologies - "Sirens and Other Demon Lovers" and "Trolls Eye View".

Wendy teaches sculpting, doll and model making and mask making workshops incorporating mythic and faery imagery and meditation. Her recent project, The Heart of Faerie Oracle -is a deck of oracle cards with book, illustrated by Brian Froud and written by Wendy Froud. This was published in March of 2010.

Wendy and Brian released a new book in September (2012). The Title is "Trolls" and it combines painting and drawing by Brian, models by Wendy and text, including stories, tale fragments and troll facts, by Wendy. It is published by Abrams. Wendy and Brian also released a series of meditation apps with music, for Iphone and Ipad. in the Autumn (2012).

Wendy has exhibited in Museums and galleries in the U.S., U.K., Europe and Japan and her work is in private collections throughout the world. She is an Academician of the British SouthWest Academy of Fine and Applied Arts.

Publisher of Faeries' Tales - http://www.abramsbooks.com

Faeries as a Personification of Nature

Whether you believe that faeries are real or imagined, their beauty touches the heart, sparks joy within, and inspires us to protect nature and the natural world -by Serene Conneeley

Since my collaboration with a friend on The Book of Faery Magic, I've been asked several times, in tones ranging from politely curious to downright rude, how I could write a book about faeries when I don't believe they physically exist. Some people have also been shocked that I would publicly admit such a thing, which makes me smile, for among much of society it's considered strange to believe that faeries do exist.

But others have thanked me for vocalising this perspective, because they too love the fae, and surrounding themselves with pictures, jewellery and clothes that evoke them, yet they aren't comfortable with the idea of winged beings, and can't believe they really exist. The imagination is a powerful, wonderful, beautiful thing, bringing richness and wonder to our lives, and we can still love faeries even if we don't consider them real physical beings.

I've always loved faeries. As a child I adored the magical tales I found in books, the puffy tulle skirts and flower tiaras I wore to ballet class, and the hours I spent outside in nature, building tiny faery houses and hoping that one day I'd catch a glimpse of a little winged creature within.

Today I still love reading magical stories of enchanted realms, dressing as a faery now and then, hanging paintings of the fae on my walls to inspire me when I write, and being outside in nature feeling myself as a part of the earth. I love the imagery, the legends and the sense of beauty and magic that faeries symbolise, and their reminder to be playful, light of heart and in love with the environment. The very idea of them lifts the spirits, and opens the heart and the mind to the potential of living a magical life.

And regardless of whether they are "real" or not, their energy exists because we want it to, because we have created them and given power to the idea of them – we have made them real. We know what they look like, what they want, what they hope for the human world. They leap out of paintings with joy and child-like abandon (although, as they represent the era in which they are painted, there are often darker faeries too, expressing the world's fears through the ages, of war, industrialisation, nuclear devastation). They come to vivid life in movies and television shows with amazing effects and messages of magic, and they twist their way into our hearts in stories brimming with imagination and enchantment, books that hold truths about life despite being fiction.

Faeries mean such different things to different people anyway, which is part of what makes them so magical and mysterious, and also what makes it a moot point whether we "believe" or not. For what definition of the fae should we believe? To some people faeries are actual physical beings, supernatural creatures with colourful wings that we can see and interact with, touch and speak to. To others they are not physical beings but etheric ones, existing in another dimension, and only able to communicate with us mind-to-mind. To still others they are simply an energy, a shimmer of sparkling light in the corner of their eye, or perhaps the soul or consciousness of a flower or tree.

For other people, faeries come to them as the spirits of departed loved ones or ancestors, more heart-centred sensation than physical reality. And there are those too who believe the fae are a race of ancient deities diminished in stature and power by more recent gods, such as the goddess Maeve's transformation in the Christian era to the far less powerful faery Mab, or the trickster god Loki being reborn as the mischievous imp Puck (as well as becoming a villainous superhero in the current Marvel film franchise).

THE FAE – SYMBOL OF NATURE

Then there are those, like me, who see the fae as the anthropomorphication of nature, our way of humanising the environment around us and understanding it in human terms. It's so easy to feel the magic of nature – and imagine fae beings – in the faery glens and faery hills of Ireland, at Findhorn in Scotland, the sacred springs of England, the enchanted forest of Broceliande in France, in ancient woodlands, tropical rainforests, undisturbed lakes and streams, moss-covered stones and ivy-clad oaks, national parks and vast deserts all over this beautiful planet, as well as in our own backyards. As writer Douglas Adams says: "Isn't it enough to see that a garden is beautiful, without having to believe that there are fairies at the bottom of it too?"

This world is so breathtakingly beautiful all on its own that we don't need supernatural beings to make flowers grow, colour a rainbow or bring beauty to a forest. As biologist and nature lover Richard Dawkins so eloquently states: "The real world, as understood scientifically, has a magic of its own – the kind I call poetic magic; an inspiring beauty which is all the more magical because it is real and because we can understand how it works."

One of the things I most love about faeries is that we have made them a personification and symbol of environmental protection and our need to love and protect our world, and a reminder to connect more often with nature and the earth. We have appointed them as the guardians of the earth, and of nature, but it is us who must actually do the work, us who must protect the forests and the endangered animals, the life-giving land, the precious water and the very air itself, to conserve our resources, care for the planet, and speak out when those in power seek to destroy it – oh so necessary for us with our current government especially. We must live in harmony with nature, consider it sacred, and work with it rather than against it.

So rather than leaving the responsibility of caring for the environment to creatures that may or may not exist, it's important to me that we step up. That we clean up the beaches, parks and forests, that we bring awareness to environmental issues, reduce our usage, recycle what we can, raise money for eco causes, teach our children to value the earth and not take it for granted. That when we see a problem in the world, we take steps to address it, no matter how small those steps might seem or what form the issues that concern us might take

BRINGING THE JOY OF THE FAE INTO OUR LIVES

Living life inspired by our idea of faeries, of their light-hearted and child-like innocence and way of seeing the world, can also bring us great joy. They remind us to not take life too seriously, to not take things personally, to find time to play, to remember what it was like to be a child, and to see the world filled with unlimited potential and possibility. I always seem to have a million deadlines and work too long and too hard, so reminding myself to connect with my inner faery, the child-like part of me that remembers the importance of play, is vital to me. I don't have to believe they are real to be inspired by the energy they embody, to remind myself to bring a little levity and laughter to my life.

It's easy to add a little fae energy to your life – you can start by simply remembering what you loved doing when you were a kid, and doing it now. Go play on the swings or feed the ducks (I visit our neighbourhood ducks and swamp hens quite often, and watching them swimming and squawking and wiggling their bottoms in the air when they dive underwater always makes me smile). Get a hula hoop, some elastics or a skipping rope, and reconnect with the joy of movement. Fly a kite, have a costume party, or spend a day at an amusement park and nurture your inner child. Watch a kids' TV show or movie without feeling you have to justify it to anyone. Finger paint, bake a faery cake or wear a faery dress to work. (It will not only lift your spirits, but those around you too.)

Follow your passion, whatever that is. Do something unexpected and fun and playful and wild, and start to tune in to what it is you love to do, rather than the things that are expected of you. This is not about shirking responsibility or running away from your grown-up life, but simply finding time to be light and happy, to connect to your joyful heart and remember to enjoy this amazing life we are all so blessed to be living.

So no, I don't think it's essential to "believe" in faeries to write about them, to invoke the light-hearted energy we've assigned to them or to channel their inspiration – many of the most amazing faery artists and authors don't think they physically exist, but are enchanted by the idea of them, and love to embody their energy on canvas or on the page, helping us all connect with the inspiration that flows through from the myths and legends and stories of the fae.

Likewise many of those working to preserve the earth – from wisdom keepers and environmental groups to the individuals who protest about logging, plant trees, write about global warming and sail pirate ships on the high seas to save the whales – don't believe in literal supernatural beings, but take on the role we've attributed to the faeries, turning the passion, wisdom and eco awareness we credit faeries with into real and powerful human action.

Ultimately it doesn't matter whether you believe faeries are fact or fiction, but what you do with your life, how much magic you allow into it, and whether your actions embody the best of what we attribute to the fae – living with joy and wonder, having a kind and loving heart, maintaining a child-like wonder at the world, and caring about nature and the earth.

Serene Conneeley is the author of six books, including Seven Sacred Sites, A Magical Journey and Into the Mists. She is the editor of several children's magazines – which gives her reason to play – and is currently working on her next novel. Visit her at SereneConneeley.com.

Lunar New Year – The Year of the Wood Horse

Artwork Credit – Nicolle Poll

Embracing the Year of the Wood Horse, Nicolle Poll gives an insight of the energies it brings on what promises to be a dynamic, fast paced and fortuitous year ahead…

Welcome to the 2014 Lunar Year of the Wood Horse also known as the Year of the Green Horse. Based on the Chinese Lunar Calendar, Chinese New Year commences on the new moon of 31st January 2014 and ends on 18th February 2015. According to the Chinese Horoscope Stem-Branch Calendar the Wood Horse Year begins 4th February 2014, though many communities will begin celebrating the Wood Horse Year on the Chinese New Year.

The Horse is the seventh sign of the Chinese Zodiac which consists of twelve animal signs. Each sign is featured for a year, creating a twelve year cycle for the zodiac to progress through all the signs. Within each animal sign, there is a cycle of the five elements; metal, water, wood, fire and earth. Within this cycle, it takes sixty years before the same animal sign and element to be experienced again, with the last Wood Horse cycle being in 1954. Wood is the element of Spring, representing new growth and is connected to trees and the colour green, hence the reference to Wood and Green Horse. It is also associated with creativity, with a seed being planted something new will emerge. It is a time of coming together collectively and helping each other towards a higher purpose.

A person born in the Wood Horse Year is known to be reasonable, stable and strong, adaptable to change and good at making decisions. Interacting well with others, they do well in professional and personal relationships, and these aspects can be applied to the energy of the year.

The positive aspect of this Wood Horse Year brings with it a cycle for powerful and dynamic times by mixing the fixed fire element in its sign with the current wood year cycle. Horses are known for their speed and agility, so be on the ready for exciting opportunities that come quickly and for things to come and go rapidly.

Enjoy lucky breaks, and if back luck occurs, the Wood Horse energy will soften these blows. This is the time to take more chances and risks than you normally would, striking out in new directions with more confidence and making major changes in your life. Energy is high and productivity is rewarded. This is the year for decisive action that brings about results; however it is important to only do so when it intuitively feels right.

The Wood Horse Year is also about adventure, connecting to nature, travel and personal freedom. If you find yourself in a personally restrictive situation, the Horse encourages you to find a way to be creative with expressing your personal freedom within those boundaries. If travelling, roaming to places far away and off the beaten path will be most rewarding.

Personal relationships flourish and deepen under the Wood Horse sign, helping to strengthen ties and enjoy healthy boundaries and connections. It is a good time to bring issues out in the open, especially with family.

The shadow side aspect of the Wood Horse Year brings the caution of not rushing in where wise men fear to tread. Though considered a year of favourable luck, make sure to use commonsense and due diligence in your actions. If you are not 100% sure about a decision, don't do it. With events in a Horse Year moving quickly, ensure you don't gallop off in the wrong direction or you can end up broke by the end of the year. Be aware that overspending and impulse buying is strong in a Horse Year, and the short term pleasure derived can affect your long term planning.

The impulsive ways of a Horse Year is not for everyone. The opposite sign of the Horse is the Rat, these ways can bring challenges to Rat's considered and well planned approach to life. For Rat and Ox Signs, you will benefit more from going with the flow, being thrifty and consolidating on what you already have and let those compatible with the Horse be the risk takers. The signs compatible with the Horse are Tiger, Dog and Sheep. Denial of problems is another shadow aspect of the Horse sign, be mindful to wrap loose ends, clean up your own messes and pay attention to details.

A Horse Year often ends either with triumph or tragedy, so use the Horse Wood Year energy wisely. If you do, your year ahead will be one of freedom, instinctiveness, responding quickly to opportunity with rapid results, enjoying breakthroughs and moments for personal and professional success, connecting to nature, enjoying life's adventures and a time to leap and soar.

Nicolle Poll is a regular contributor and part of the inSpirit creative team. Nicolle works as an Artist specialising in Oracle Cards, Totemic Animal illustrations and Soul Journey portraits, also having studied and practised a wide range of modalities in her personal and spiritual development.

Contact Nicolle at: Email: artworkbynicolle@bigpond.com or **Facebook:** www.facebook.com/ArtworkByNicolle

The Magic of the Sacred Stones

Kye Crow delves into the ancient world of Sacred Stone magic, sharing the knowledge of the Ghoumas and how their wisdom guides our path with the Fae…

I grew up in the English countryside with its rambling roses and hawthorn blossoms, bright yellow buttercups and big red clovers buzzing with bees, and from an early age I was enchanted by the Fae.

My favourite book was the Flower Fairies by Cicely Mary Barker and my most secret yearning was to talk with the animals, just like my hero, Dr Doolittle.

I had no idea how as an adult, these worlds would merge as I learnt to communicate with the animals and work with the Fae in helping traumatised and frightened animals that arrived at our sanctuary.

Often it was the Fae that would guide me to an animal that needed help, a baby bird that had fallen out of its nest, an eagle with an injured wing. I felt as if I was following an invisible chord of light that would guide me through the woods and have me wading through streams, wherever I needed to go to reach the animal I was meant to find.

I soon discovered that the Fae honour those that care for the animals and walk gently upon Mother Earth. When we do this all the elemental realms are open to us, the tree spirits, the guardians of the crystals, the dragons and one of my favourites, the sacred stones.

Living in the desert and caring for wildlife I have been blessed in getting to know many animals well.

One of these is the Emu, one of the guardians of the Ghoumas, the small stones that love to travel and they find the most magical ways to do so. I have no idea where the name Ghouma originates from, but I have known them by this name for over twenty years.

The Ghoumas have many different purposes and some, who live in the desert where there is little rain, will be carried to a waterhole by Emu, who swallows them as an aid to digestion.

Once they have passed through emu's system they may sit at that waterhole soaking up the water for many years to come. That is how long it takes for them to absorb the moisture. Rocks are much more porous than we think!

When Emu swallows them again and carries them back out into the desert and drops them off, they are like a rain magnet, because like attracts like and all that moisture they have soaked up over the years, draws in the clouds and creates a storm.

Other Ghoumas serve to protect and like me, you may have found yourself feeling compelled to pick up a stone and carry it with you or even give it to someone in need, without knowing why. Even the most powerful wizard will not go near someone under the protection of a Ghouma.

Another love of mine is the stone circles of my homeland and I have spent much time in ritual amongst them. Like they are kin the Ghoumas, they also soak up and transmit energy. Priests and priestesses sitting in different circles many miles apart can use the energy of the earth and the frequencies of the stones to communicate with one another.

The stones are also guardians of the dragons, who for many years as our earth moved through darkness, went deep into our earth to hibernate. People forgot that all life was sacred. They forgot they were spiritual beings and they violated the divine right of animals to co-exist in peace. They even plundered the very earth that gave them nourishment and life.

All the Sacred Realms began to withdraw; the Fae went deeper into the forests and found more remote locations, the dragons dug even deeper into the earth, some even hid themselves in the rocks and mountains. The animals stopped communicating and all these magical realms were delegated to the world of fantasy and a vivid imagination.

But the times are changing. More of us choose to honour and walk our sacred path. To choose love, no matter what, the still sleeping dragons are stirring deep below the earth, stretching from their slumbers, as they too awaken. Every time we stop to help an injured bird or refuse to support industries that profit from the suffering of animals, our own connection to the Sacred Realms of the animals grows stronger. Every time we plant a tree, or choose to buy organic or stand up to stop our old forests being logged, we open up magical doorways that enables us to connect with the Fae.

Kye Crow is the Creatress of Wunjo Crow, a range of Goddess clothing that's sprinkled with love and sewn with magic. Kye and her partner Gill live with over a 100 rescued animals and teach Sacred Journeys into the Animal Realms, the power of Love and how to live on planet earth as a sensitive.

Contact Kye at: Web: www.camelcampsanctuary.com / Facebook: www.facebook.com/Wunjocrow

Photo Credit: Argnesh Rose Visionary Digital Artist specialising in fantasy and totem portraiture – www.givethemwings.com.au

Wisdom from the Fae

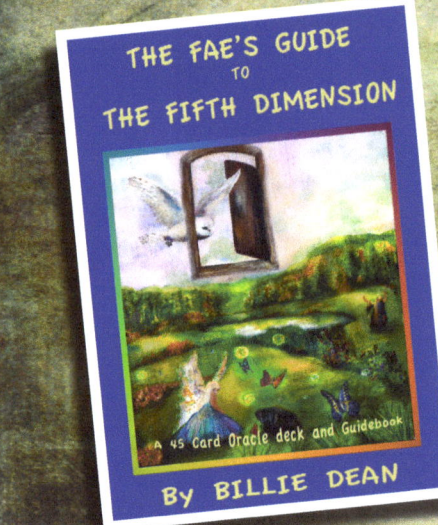

Billie Dean gives voice to the Fae as they share much needed teachings for the evolution of ourselves, and of how our lives and world could be…

WALKING ACROSS THE PADDOCK AT DUSK, ALONE WITH MY THOUGHTS AND MY DOGS, I WAS SHOCKED WHEN A MAN SUDDENLY APPEARED RIGHT IN FRONT OF ME.

Before I had a chance to speak, he placed his hands on my shoulders, looked me squarely in the eye and said: "Write."

And then he disappeared.

It was the first time this particular teacher from the fae realms had left our sacred spot where he usually taught me, hunkered down around a fire amidst some old Elm trees. It was a place where the dimensions met.

I grinned. There's always a sense of "something bigger" when a fae man yells at you. Lean and tall, wearing a shirt and breeches, this one was handsome, sweet, funny and wise. He also spoke in mysterious riddles, dropping words into my consciousness for me to work out as homework. Words that were relevant to my re-membering.

For me my journey with the fae is interwoven with destiny and my spiritual journey. It's about peace for all species, the mystery path of the magical ways, and the search for happiness and abundance.

The fae I know are the "people of peace" or the "shining ones" from the ancient Celtic Tuatha de Daanan. And they were the people who, legend has it, were a magical race who "disappeared underground" when "defeated" when the Milesans invaded Ireland.

The first hint I had that I had anything to do with these particular people, were from my dog Willow, who said we were both "children of the Danu", and that she had been my teacher and I had been her teacher. She gave me a mission which sent me delving deep into the Otherworld in search of information.

It wasn't until I was soul-called to go to Ireland that the fae upped the ante. On Tara there is an ancient faerie tree, an old Hawthorn, and as I approached her, I received clear instructions on how to enter her portal. I was sucked into another time and place where all kinds of elegant folk were in a huge hall, dancing and having fun – the old fashioned way. Ballroom dancing kind of fun. Their eyes twinkled and their hearts were carefree.

"This is where you came from," said a voice. "We kicked you out to do your work. Once a bard, always a bard. Once a poet, always a poet."

I have always written. And when I was ten I announced that I would be a "writer or a vet" when I grew up. It wasn't surprising that I became a journalist who also studied alternative medicine. Nor was it a surprise to find myself living as a writer with a huge number of rescued animals who called for help because they have a soul contract with me, and because I could hear and understand their silent language.

The fae I know, are protectors of the animals, and they want us to have a paradigm shift. They dismiss terms like "ascension". They think we are all far too serious and "spotted with muck" and want us to laugh, be merry, and remember that magic is about everyone having plenty.

One day I was given a vision of a beautiful place which tugged at all the strings of my heart and soul. There was a green country meadow and gorgeous old trees, blue skies and fluffy clouds. Everything was illuminated by sparkling light, highlighted by little touches, like a wooden bridge over a bubbling brook.

I knew at once it was the land of the fae.

They asked me if I would like to go Home. I was silent. To go Home was the only thing I wanted to do. To live and love in beauty and peace among my own kind. To escape the battle field of density – the daily struggle to live in a world I clearly didn't fit.

"No," I heard myself saying. "I'm supposed to help bring Home here."

It was the first time I realised the truth of why I had incarnated here.

There are many of us from the fae realms who have come back at this time to help with the Great Shift. They may or may not know it, but they are caring for animals, and the earth, they are working as creatives and performers. No matter what they are doing, inherent to us all, is this love of nature and animals, and a desire to protect both.

To help with the great shift into the fifth dimension the fae told me to create a

DEEP PEACE FOR ALL SPECIES
28

FAERIE DOG
42

deck of cards. They even told me who the artist should be – a lovely soul and gorgeous artist called Christine Leefe who I met at one of my live events. "Faerie!" they yelled at me when it was Chris's turn to receive the Andean shaman rites. I had no idea she was an artist and her work is perfect for them. The fae told me exactly how the pictures needed to look, and gave me the words and the wisdom, and Chris did her part beautifully. I was told to always put aside the old ways and thoughts that are heavy and ponderous and keep people bound to a past no longer relevant. The one big concern was to focus on the Light. And that meant light-hearted!!

For many years now, the Good People and the animals have been sharing their advice with me about how to live better here on Earth. They say that humans tend to forget there are other species and other dimensions sharing the planet. And that we don't have enough fun. This is especially important. Fun is a key to magical living, and the higher dimensions. And without it, it's hard to get "lift off".

They say to spend time walking and dancing barefoot is essential, and that if we are to activate the new software, we must move our bodies more. Yoga is excellent. Being out in nature, drinking the sun, allowing the earth to heal you and honouring the animals. Making the home a sacred sanctuary of peace, and living life as an art form. Also high on the list is doing your work to peel off the layers of conditioning to reveal the true jewel within. This is what is so important now.

At a recent fae workshop that I gave, we were all told we had to act faster for change. It was time humans and elementals worked together for the highest good. It was time we remembered they existed.

The fae tell me it is essential people stop eating animal foods and contributing to animal suffering of any kind, and that in order to arrive at the place of beauty takes a perception and a paradigm shift. It's not about history, modern or ancient. This time is new. They said it was difficult to "get off the ground" when consuming suffering. And that in the new earth, suffering won't exist. They believe in peace for all species, and this has been the foundation of all my work.

Interestingly, I had a film crew come to interview some of the animals we have here. One big red Angus steer we call Buddha, gave me a huge nudge to get my attention. "We are the People of Peace," he said. "We are not to be eaten."

I always knew Buddha was special. But now I knew him to be one of the fae tribes. I have many animals at home, who are fae souls, here for their own soul journey, or ours.

The wisdom the fae imparted through the cards is one showing how life could be if we embraced their teachings. It portrays a wonderful, gentle world of love, friendship, harmony, self expression, great beauty and.. **deep peace for all species.**

Billie Dean is an award-winning author (Secret Animal Business) actress (Finding Joy) and animal advocate. She and her husband Andrew also write books, make independent films and perform comedy. They run A Place of Peace Farm Animal Sanctuary and have founded The Deep Peace Trust to help fund the sanctuary, and other creative initiatives for global cultural change and world peace. Billie also works as a shamanic practitioner for people and animals, is a natural animal telepath and empath and holds a vision of the future that is beautiful. Her fae cards and books are coming out in 2014. For more information or to pre buy – info@billiedean.com www.billiedean.com www.wildpureheart.com

Faery Flashback

May Gem~mer's enchanting article inSpire you to reconnect with childhood memories and early connections with the delightful Fae…

Swimming back in time through my well of memories, I recall an image of a wee little girl living in a small country village. A wee lass who spent many moments of solitude, many moments of playtime happily by herself; or seemingly so. As I tap into this imagery of my childhood memories, I see that to all the adults in the village I grew up in, that I appeared to have played on my own quite often. And the other children in the village I grew up in, well, I don't recall any of my flesh and blood little friends knowing that when I was playing in the huge mounds, mountains even, of dirt within the confines of our family land, that I was not ever by myself.

At this special time of my childhood innocence, I never really thought too much about the little people that I was building cave homes for, I just connected and played with little beings, building them little cave villages to live in and explore, carving their homes into the sides of huge gravel mounds that were frequently formed on our land by my gravel contracting parents.

Diving into the well of my memories once again, this time not having to swim back so far, I recall a special encounter that occurred in a very special and very sacred place, a place where I experienced a flashback that had me swimming within the realms of my childhood memories at a time where I so innocently and divinely connected with little people, little beings that were faery folk.

Not so long ago, I walked the shores of the amazing and energetically ancient Norah Head beaches that surrounded the equally amazing Norah Head Lighthouse. There were many amazing experiences and connections had there, some to be shared, some to be kept within the confines of my memory well, yet all to be treasured forever.

Drawn more and more every day to the ancient and fossilised energy held deep within the veins of rock formations along the coast, connecting and discovering the ancient secrets kept by rock people was beginning to play an important part in my beach journeys and my stay at Norah Head was no different. I was constantly amazed and in awe of the diverse abundance of ancient energies held within the seas and the land there, yet I found myself enthralled by the rock formations and platforms at this sacred space. As I ran my hands over rock faces, connecting and conversing, there was one day that I discovered little caves; tiny cave homes, cave villages carved out in the rock walls. I found myself dropping to me knees as I recalled creating the exact same teeny tiny cave formations when I was all but 5 years old. At that moment in time I felt connected with rock people and faery beings as they opened a portal in time when the faery folk were my guiding lights.

I flashed back to a time of innocence, a time where I spent almost every waking moment at home outside, in the dirt, with the faeries. So long ago was this time, that I had long since forgotten the connection that I shared with the fae and at the exact moment that I fell to my knees, with the images and the overwhelming feelings that washed over me, I once again acknowledged and accepted that my sweet little childhood friends were faeries, folk of the fae that had embraced me and nurtured me in my solitude and the angst of my childhood.

This flashback, the recall of connections to the faery folk in my innocent years astounded me and here I was again, surrounded by the fae who were showing me, opening me, reminding me of my deep sense of knowing. In that moment in time on the sacred shores of Norah Head, in the realms of the rock people, the faery folk delivered to me my self-trust, my full acceptance of always having been connected to the unseen, the unknown, to the other realms, to the faery folk. It was this faery flashback to my most personal and uninhibited connections to the fae that allowed me to release every single wall, barrier and inhibition that I had built up over the years, it all floated away on the wings of the fae, leaving me clear and open to seeing and allowing the amazing and true spirit that I am to shine through uninhibited once again.

Gem~mer is an Ocean Enchantress, Intuitive Creatress and Teacher of Ocean Magicks. Gem's creative works include crafting ocean talismans and tools for spiritual connections and teaching ocean magicks through magazine articles, workshops and online courses. Gem~mer has also begun the magickal journey of creating oracle and insight decks, books and birthing illuminating retreats as a way of sharing and teaching the magick and wisdom of ocean and sea's. 'May the Wisdom and Magick of Ocean and Sea's Inspire Us All'. www.cryshellmagic.com.au

Clothing from the Faerie Realm

Natasha Heard shows how to radiate positive energy and magic every day by embracing the ways and wisdom of your very own Fae style...

WANT TO FEEL FAERIE FANTASTIC EVERY DAY?

Take some inspiration from Faerie friends and be inspired to wear clothing that reflects your innermost passions, your individual Faerie style and your love of yourself and your environment.

Organic materials, rich colours, sparkling shimmers, patterns and prints! Allow your inner Fae to go wild when shopping for your Faerie wear.

I have noticed that some people wear clothes they don't really like, and continue to purchase clothes they don't like simply out of lack of passion and a lack of self-confidence, perhaps out of necessity. Feeling bored and tired of life, or always looking after the family first? They may not want to attract attention from others. This in itself is a negative cycle, a pattern of self-confidence destruction. If this is you then allow me to share some faerie tips to add a touch of magic your wardrobe.

I have been told my fashion sense is like a bag of mixed lollies; however I feel it would be more like a medicine pouch full of crystals and magical trinkets and I am sure the Fae would agree. Right now I am wearing a tie dyed green skirt made from natural hemp, it is so comfortable and it reminds me of one of my favourite crystals, Moss Agate. I wear this skirt with a soft pixie sleeve top printed with feathers and stars and a soft amethyst-purple poncho, I also have on purple socks with stars on them too! I feel like a Faerie~Crystal woman, I radiate positive energy and ooze magic wherever I go.

I am very passionate about wearing clothes that I love. I won't wear just anything and even just around my home I still wear my favourite clothes because they make me feel like me ~ magical, feminine and fun, confident and happy. If I were to wear clothes I thought were dull and ordinary than I too would feel that way, so buying and wearing clothes I love is an anti-depressant in a way. I feel an investment in clothing that resonates with my energy is so very worth every cent. I will wear these clothes till they are full of holes and I even quite like the holes! But then I may cut them up and create with them. My clothing must be in the colours I love. Purples, greens and rainbows. Tie dyed or printed with images of my animal totems or anything I am passionate about. I don't own an iron or an ironing board as I like to keep my life as stress free as possible. So my clothing must be made out of crinkle free materials and I like to wear natural fibres and clothing that feels soft and beautiful to the touch.

So go on and faerie up your wardrobe. Clear out the old, anything you don't feel passionate about should go. If it is too big or too small then give it away or you could sell your old clothes to help fund your next amazing purchase. When I look through my wardrobe I don't have an excessive amount of clothes but every item of clothing is unique and truly magical in its own way. I go through my wardrobe often and gift anything I am not resonating with anymore to charity or my friends, and I will have a fun clothing swap day. When you go shopping hold off on buying till you really feel excited about something, when that special piece catches your eye then try it on. If it is in a colour you love and it feels comfortable on, you are almost there. If you see your reflection in the mirror and see yourself smiling, your eyes shining and you feel all aglow you know you have found something special!

When you are wearing your specially chosen clothes you smile, your aura brightens and your self-confidence heightens. You will attract positivity into your life because you feel so positive! You radiate love and light and therefore it returns to you three fold. This may seem basic but it is powerful faerie magic.

Here are some of my favorite links to magical faerie fashions; a lot of this clothing is made by my faerie friends who connect deeply with and love our Mother Earth with passion and it resonates with all their creations.

SCARLETTE ROSE FAERIE
http://stores.ebay.com.au/scarlette-rose-fairy - E-bay shop.

WUNJO CROW
https://www.facebook.com/Wunjocrow - Facebook page.

WYLDESKY
https://www.etsy.com/au/shop/Wyldeskye - Etsy Shop

FOLK OWL
http://www.etsy.com/uk/shop/folkowl - Etsy shop.

ZIZZYFAE ~ www.zizzyfay.com - website.

*Natasha Heard is a creatress of all things magical! A natural witch ~ her magical life and connection to the Earth flow into all her creations. Specialising in Wands, Sceptres and Staves; and creating with her horticulturalist husband Michael, Blessed Rune sets and Tree of Life Bind Rune Talismans. Her innate connection with all aspects of the natural world and passion for magic is what makes her a true creatress of powerful, magical tools. Natasha can be contacted at: www.blessedbranches.com
Email: blessedbranches@gmail.com or flowerlove@live.com.au / Facebook: Blessed Branches...magical tools by Natasha Heard.*

Faery Messages

THERE ARE MANY THINGS IN LIFE THE HUMAN EYE CANNOT SEE. IT DOES NOT MEAN THAT OTHER LIFE BEYOND OUR SENSES DOES NOT EXIST. IT IS POSSIBLE THAT THERE ARE OTHER PLANES OF EXISTENCE WHERE OTHER BEINGS RESIDE. THERE ARE MANY SCHOOLS OF THOUGHT ABOUT WHETHER FAERIES EXIST. THERE ARE SO MANY COUNTRIES WITH FAERY FOLKLORE THAT STARTED LONG BEFORE INTERCONTINENTAL TRAVEL, THAT YOU HAVE TO PONDER HOW SO MANY STORIES COME ABOUT OF THE 'WEE' PEOPLE.

Are they merely nature spirits showing themselves to us in a very non-threatening way by looking human-like? Or is it just a way we daydream and wish for some magic and an escape from the everyday life? I see faeries when I meditate and they pass very important messages onto me. So are they real or just a way for my own soul to communicate to me in pictures? I have Celtic ancestry in my blood, could this be why I am drawn to them and communicate with them? To be honest, I'm not quite sure. I would love to know they are real and certainly open to it regardless of what people think of me. I still would like to be able to see them with my own eyes, but maybe that is just a lot harder due to our physical make-up? Whether they do or don't exist really is irrelevant. It's one of those debates that could possibly go on for centuries and I don't care much for debates that can't be proven.

What we need to pay attention to is the common themes and messages we receive from them. The messages come from a place of vast, ancient earth knowledge, which still applies to us today, probably even more so now than ever. Their messages are of Peace, Love, Trust and most importantly to look after and protect our environment. Who knows, it may be the earth itself trying to communicate to us. I am grateful for my communication with the Fae and so I wanted to share with you some of the messages I have received from them. Sometimes I meditate and meet them and sometimes it's through automatic drawing, something I was amazed to discover I could do. When I automatic draw them, they just spring to life on the page and in a completely different drawing style than I normally use. I get an image and feeling and then I receive their name. It's like opening a portal to receive a whisper.

THE FAERY CRONE - A wise old lady. Do not let her looks be deceiving, she may hobble about, but when you are not looking she flits about with lightning speed. She may or may not give you advice, but when she does, you'd better hang on for the ride. Her truth can propel you forward in a blink of an eye.

I have met the Fairy Crone on a few occasions in meditations. She was hobbling about really slow when I first met her and when I turned away, I saw her dash about out the corner of my eye. She took my hand and off we flew so fast I could barely see where we were going. We flew down a hole at the base of tree next to a creek. We flew through a labyrinth of underground caves and holes with lots of faeries peering out trying to see what the fuss was about and chittering to themselves. Then as fast as we were underground, we popped up out of another tree at the edge of a waterfall. She then so matter-of-factly threw me off the edge and said, "It's time to fly!" I thought I would fall, but I didn't. I was floating. She had shown me that she knew I was ready, I just needed the push.

"Be still, be quiet, open your mind and allow yourself to see the beauty of something unnoticed."

GODDESS INSPIRATION
Aine

THE FAERY GODDESS OF LOVE, HARMONY & FERTILITY.

Aine is a Celtic Goddess of Irish origin. She was associated with both the sun and moon in her lifetimes and is still honored during the Summer Solstice in some countries. Aine was said to be exceedingly friendly with human men and is said to have given birth to many magickal Faerie/Human beings. One of her many aspects was her command over crops and animals and was apparently able to shapeshift to animal form as a red mare.

Aine is also referred to being Merlin's Lady of the Lake. She appeared to men as a woman of great beauty and was said to have spellbound them. She is often invoked to perform love spells, bring fertility, faery magic, prosperity and for keeping vows. She is said to protect women and if needed you only need to ask for her and the faeries help. She will give you strength and courage and guard you against harm. She is also known to love silver and white items, so these are also good to use when invoking her presence.

DENVER THE OAK GUARDIAN - I met Denver when doing a meditation from The Pathways to Faery app by The Frouds. Denver was the little guardian that appeared to open the doorway into another world through the Oak Tree. He will only show himself if you come with an open heart and will do no harm. Otherwise he will not even show himself. He is a friendly little fellow.

THE WEAVER - I first took the picture of the fungus on the side of a very old tree in Tasmania. Only to find that when I looked at it on the computer, I noticed what appeared to be a face in the hole peering out. When I drew the faery and spider on the fungus, it was merely to represent youth in training. When I meditated on this card, I ventured inside the hole to find an ancient spider, a weaver of the threads of time. She showed me my loom. At the beginning it was all woven together showing my past already completed. Then there were two single threads showing two different outcomes because the future is always changing. But here I was cutting one thread that went downhill to leave the remaining thread which went upwards. On this thread were symbols - a love heart, a dollar sign and a plane. I had chosen a path that will bring me love, money and travel. So now I see The Weaver as an Oracle.

ANCIENT WISDOM

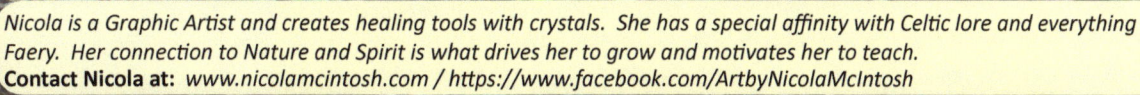

Whatever you believe, remember there is so much more to the workings of nature that man does not yet understand. Spirit comes in many forms.

Nicola is a Graphic Artist and creates healing tools with crystals. She has a special affinity with Celtic lore and everything Faery. Her connection to Nature and Spirit is what drives her to grow and motivates her to teach.
Contact Nicola at: www.nicolamcintosh.com / https://www.facebook.com/ArtbyNicolaMcIntosh

Magical Realms

LAURA NAOMI SHARES HER CONNECTION WITH OTHERWORLDLY REALMS, AND EXPLAINS HOW IMPORTANT IT IS TO UNDERSTAND YOUR OWN UNIQUE BONDS WITH THESE MAGICAL WORLDS...

SHAMANISM

UPON WAKING I SEE A SOFT GLOW OF MAGICAL BEINGS GENTLY FADING INTO THE ONCOMING DAWN. MY BODY IS TINGLING AND I FEEL LIKE I'VE BEEN TICKLED BY FEATHERS AND I KNOW I HAVE BEEN COMMUNING WITH THE FAERIES AGAIN.

A connection with the magical realms has always been interwoven in my dreaming and how I exist in the spiritual worlds. This refined cosmic energy always acts as a reminder and stirs the threads of magic in the veins of our existence.

Discussions were often held about encounters with otherworldly beings and I was encouraged to continue open communication and psychic interaction with the energies that came into my field. Without me consciously realising it as a child, this offered not just the lighter energies but also the darker energies to reveal themselves. It was quite frightening sometimes and eventually I decided to express through creativity rather than speaking about it. My communication was through energy; feeling, music, art and being an interpreter. These experiences helped me define and attune my psychic senses consciously to the multitude of dimensions that exist. In fact, it seemed more real to me than the waking world – it made more sense what was revealed and shared with me through these other languages. I listened to the quiet hum of the stars, the silky voices of a stream, whispers in the wind, and the secret sighs of the night. I would lie on the Earth and feel the union of laughter of the grasses moving around me, I'd hear the soft murmurs of the leaves dancing in the breeze speaking about the edges of the universe. This connection is what fills my every sense of being.

The door to the magical realms was always wide open and I came to eventually realise, the reason for the bonds with other worlds.

I remember very clearly as a child visiting a crystal shop and the woman behind the counter gazed at me inquisitively saying "Oh dear one, you have them lining up to speak to you!" I replied with a silent shyness, and then she continued "Remember, there is a reason for the gifts you have." The moment seemed to suspend in time and indeed a gentle light and sparkling eyes reminded me of her words.

It wasn't until I was about 18 years old, I started to really discover the reason for the otherworldly energy. I came to know the magical aspects of myself and how this energy was being channeled into this world. In healings, ceremony or spiritual guidance, my magical connections have come to aid in the process. In a lot of these other realms, time does not exist and the space is very different; these types of energies continue a healing or integration process even if the person (physical body) has left the session. It is common to hear people comment about how time seems to stand still or cease to exist in the sacred space we create for healings or ceremony.

Faeries, elves, angels, light beings and other beings are often spiritual helpers and guides. In Shamanism we work with these energies, which are in harmony with nature and the Earth. An example is faery energy – it is subtle yet incredibly powerful and is very fluent energy that heals fractured space. Faery energy has different aspects; very mischievous and playful, gentle and innocent and also sensual and majestic. It's about knowing what type of energy is required; its appropriateness and when it needs to be called upon.

Most magical creatures I've encountered have a purpose, much like how we each have a purpose and unique gifts. When clearing energy, journeying into other realms or facilitating a healing, often my helpers travel with me and engagements with beings are frequent.

Communication is displayed in various forms; sometimes in very abstract ways, there's a cleverness and an ethereal intelligence, and is truly exquisite. In Shamanic societies, these magical links are encouraged as each of us have innate relationships to certain otherworldly realms. We are interdimensional beings and our interdimensional connections bring through specific energy onto this planet. In my experience it's about learning how to filter these energies onto this earthly plane and knowing why you have these unions. Our otherworldly families allow us to visit this energy to restore and remember our interdimensional consciousness.

Laura Naomi is a Contemporary Shaman, which blends the unique modalities of Zen practices, Shamanic and energy healing, space clearing and psychic and emotional counselling. She guides individuals, groups, corporations and businesses and is passionate about creating more awareness around energy and the spiritual world; how it affects us and how to harness this power to create a more harmonious lifestyle. - Contact Lani Neilson @ Lani Neilson: www.lanineilson.com.au

Contact Laura at: Web: www.laura-naomi.com / **Email:**   yourdreams@globaldreamwhisperer.com / **Phone:**   1300 887 581

The Swan Blessing
RELEASING THE VOW TO NEVER LIFT THE VEIL TO THE OTHERWORLD

With the final vow concluding this fascinating series of freeing the binds of past life vows and beliefs, Julia Inglis brings understanding as to how Sacred Vows taken in previous times can affect your current life, and most importantly, how you can release this binding…

At the start of every Swan Blessing session we travel in shamanic journeying through an ancient forest to a deep a dreaming pool. This pool acts as a sacred threshold. A point of crossing from the mundane world into the Dreaming, into the Otherworld. At first the reflection of the pool's surface acts as a mirror to show you how you look now and then this reflection shifts and changes as we call to the spirit of the past life self that is being held by the binding of past life promises, vows or sacred contracts.

It is at this point of crossing the threshold that I will know very quickly if a Vow to Never Lift the Veil of Consciousness of the Otherworld has been taken. The Vow may not have been worded like that; in fact what may have been promised was to close down The Sight, the Medicine or the Gift. Or perhaps, in the past due to the heavy influence of religion, the journeyer had promised to never open the Door to Spirit or the Otherworld because they had been told it was accessing evil or danger. All of these beliefs and promises can act as a strong block when trying to access and open the Third Eye.

I believe that when we open the Third Eye we are opening not something that is forbidden or special to the lucky few, but something that is our Birthright. We are opening All of Our Eyes. The Third Eye is an eye that can see many realms and dimensions at once and I believe it is our natural gift and we have the right to reclaim and regain this access and way of seeing All That Is.

Once the binding upon this Door is released, we are able to access not only our Past Life stories, but also to see other dimensions including the realm of the Fae. My Irish grandmothers would call this these beings An Sidhe. They believed the Faeriekind to be very different from the Disneyisation we have known through television and animation. To our ancestors, the An Sidhe are an otherworldly race of beings that work closely with the Elements and the Laws of Nature and can be of great assistance to us when we too begin to co-create with Mother Earth. We are seeing these helpful spirits being accessed again more and more within the growing Biodynamic movement, a movement of wellness that actively promotes and engages in communication with Faeries to help them receive information about growing the healthiest and most sustainable gardens.

We are at a time when the Veils are thinning between the worlds. I believe it is because we are in need of the ancient wisdom held by the many beings of the Otherworld to help us bring balance and harmony to the Earth and her people again. Due to heavy religious beliefs, laws and vows and also the binding belief that you could not be a follower of Science and Magic – that you somehow had to choose one instead of the other, many of us have had little or no access to the Spirit world for many lifetimes. It is my greatest joy to see many healers and artists and mothers and fathers consciously releasing the Vow to Never Lift the Veil and removing the Oath to Close the Third Eye at this time of powerful awakening. When All of our Eyes are open we can heal a part of ourselves that has always known the Otherworld exits but felt separated and blocked from accessing it and also gain the gift of ancient wisdom and teachings that can help us to heal ourselves and the Earth again.

Swan Blessing Shamanic Past Life unbinding sessions are offered both in person and by Skype. Please contact Julia at tribe@sacredfamiliar.com.au or phone 0421 249 183 to book.

For the love of Angels

By Susanne Hartas

THE ARCHANGELS GUIDE AND PROTECT THE 'NATURE ANGELS' OR 'ELEMENTALS' WHO LIVE AMONG THE NATURAL WORLD OF FLOWERS, TREES, WATER, ROCKS AND SOIL. NATURE ANGELS ARE KNOWN BY MANY NAMES INCLUDING FAIRIES, DEVAS, ELVES AND SPRITES AND THEY WORK IN PARTNERSHIP WITH THE ARCHANGELS IN PROTECTING AND RESTORING MOTHER EARTH. THESE MAGICAL NATURE SPIRITS HAVE EXCEPTIONAL HEALING ABILITIES AND THEY STRIVE TO MAINTAIN BALANCE AND HARMONY BETWEEN THE NATURAL WORLD AND HUMANKIND.

Archangel Ariel is a powerful 'Angel of Nature' and she can act as an angelic liaison for those who wish to connect with the Elemental Kingdom. One of Ariel's primary roles is guardian of Mother Earth and with the assistance of the 'Nature Angels' she inspires human beings to appreciate and take care of our precious planet.

There is an Archangel assigned to govern each element and the group of elementals associated with it. Archangel Michael is guardian of the Fire element, that provides the spark for all life, and he oversees the fire spirits known as Salamanders. Archangel Gabriel defends the element of Water and cares for the water spirits known as Undines. While Archangel Uriel protects the Earth element and guides the Earth spirits, who work close to the surface of Earth being Fairies, Elves and Gnomes and Archangel Raphael is the protector of the Air element and manages the Air spirits who live high in the mountains known as Sylphs.

The Archangels message -

"Lay within the arms of 'Mother Earth', feel her embrace for she offers much love, nourishment and support. For it is within the scent of a flower, the breeze of the ocean, the softness of grass beneath your feet and the warmth of the sun surrounding your body is where comfort of her arms may be felt and this truly is the expression of the Divine's love radiating forth for you. Many blessings, Beloved Ones."

Susanne Hartas is a Psychic Medium and Angel Intuitive.

Please contact Susanne at:
www.inspiritmagazine.com
mail@inspiritmagazine.com

Faery Files:

Radio Host to the Paranormal, Alex Cayas investigates as to why the Faery Realm has been left to be by those who seek to uncover…

In 1917 in the small English village of Cottingley, two cousins took the first of five photographs that would inspire wonder and divide opinion of their authenticity for over 60 years. The tale of the Cottingley Faeries caught the interest of leading thinkers and researchers of the time, the press, the public, poets and authors such as Sir Arthur Conan Doyle. Now in 2014, it has caught my interest. As producer and host of Ghosts of Oz we have featured and dived into weird and wonderful stories and ideas from around the globe and even a few out of this realm. I soon realised that in our vast conversations with all sorts of folks that not one conversation or include any Faery hunters or pixie investigators. Sure we had heard terms like elementals and land spirits but no one trying to capture evidence of Faery life.

To dive right into the question I asked Rob Morphy writer for Mysterious Universe and a co-founder of American Monsters website why in his opinion we don't have paranormal teams who while hunting ghosts and tracking yowies every now and then gather for a Faery hunt

> "… one of the main reasons why ostensibly serious paranormal investigators tend to steer clear of cases involving Faeries and their ilk (be they a sprite, pixie, elf, imp, brownie, puck or leprechaun) is the fact that supposedly magical beings are steeped in folklore with very little tangible evidence of their existence."

What about personal experience? In modern paranormal investigation its often personal experience and events that take place when the camera's are off that move an investigator to delve a little deeper. "Basically the general (and oft times negatively stereotypical) opinion seems to be that those who have run-ins with genuine Tinkerbelles are glassy-eyed, ex-hippies smothered in patchouli and crystals who spend most of their leisure time dancing on ley lines and talking to tree spirits. In a field of study already assailed by skeptics and laymen alike, these types of cases usually only serve to exacerbate the scorn already heaped upon paranormal investigators… and trust me when I say they're already hefting a heavy burden.

But is an attempt to preserve one's already dubious reputation as a scientific observer of strange phenomenon a good enough reason not to investigate these cases? No. Not if the eyewitness or anecdotal evidence is solid enough, but how often is that the case? It would seem that with one glaring exception, the answer would have to be 'very rarely'."

A glaring exception as mentioned earlier was the Cottingley photos, as first glance Morphy admits "…that it is difficult to look at the Cottingley photos and not shake one's head with incredulity. They appear to be what disbelievers have always claimed they were; two-dimensional cut-outs hovering over vanity pictures of frolicking girls… Nevertheless, their admission (that the all but one of the photos were faked) effectively doomed the Cottingley photographs (much like the notorious 'Surgeon's Photo' of the Loch Ness Monster) to the nebulous void of frauds, shams and hoaxes, where they linger to this day."

On the case of the Cottingley photographs and the scope of the public reaction and interest I am reminded of the Shane Koyczan poem 'Atlantis' and the line 'Their willingness to believe, was greater than their determination to dismiss'. This doesn't answer why we don't have Faery hunters or paranormal teams sitting in circles of mushrooms for hours at a time to capture data or why faery tales are left on the shelf for bedtime stories and not used as a first clue for serious paranormal research.

"Maybe there really is something to these stories. Maybe the Cottingley photos are genuine and the girls (at that point elderly ladies) just got so weary of being hounded by the press and paranormalists that the conspired amongst themselves to come out as amateur con-artists in the hopes of finally putting the whole thing to rest. Who knows? But, until I come face to face with a sparkling, bi-winged humanoid, I'm going to chalk the whole dang thing up to relic memories of Homo Floresiensis and leave it for the next guy to figure out" says Morphy.

Like in many paranormal cases the details seem to draw us back in to the story and in true paranormal investigation we have more questions than answers. This seems ok, at least for now, as questions move us to venture out and explore these ideas where as answers sit on the shelf next to books that neatly end with happily ever after.

Alex Cayas is radio host, producer and freelance journalist. You can connect with Alex on Twitter @AlexCayas, and at Ghosts of Oz, Alex and Bec Up Late, SYD2030 and The Drive – all on Facebook.

Fairies, Gods, Aliens and Jesters: Abstruse Connections

Brendan D. Murphy investigates unexplained beings that have made themselves known throughout time from ancient to modern civilisations around the world and what research has discovered about the common link of their appearances and their messages…

In Nottingham, England, September 1979, a group of children between eight and ten years old, saw in a park "around sixty little men, about half as tall as themselves." The little men, who wore "blue tops and yellow tights" as well as jester-style caps with a bobble on the end, had wrinkled faces and long white beards with red tips. In the drawings the children did of them, as in the verbal descriptions, they greatly resemble fairies, imps, elves, dwarves, or *clowns as they might have been portrayed in the Middle Ages*, but with one jarring anachronistic detail: they were driving around in small motor cars, two men to a car. Although silent, the cars moved fast and could jump over obstructions.

This automotive jester theme repeats itself elsewhere. For example, in the 1940s a Cornish girl and her older sisters awoke in their bedroom during the night to hear a buzzing noise (though one sister reported "music and bells"). Looking out of the window they saw a "little man in a tiny red car driving around in circles." He was about eighteen inches tall, and had a white beard and a "red droopy hat." After a while, the entity just disappeared.[1]

Suggestively, many of Dr. Rick Strassman's DMT study participants in America in the 1990s encountered beings they perceived as clowns, jokers, jesters or imps whilst in their psychedelically altered states. At least half encountered some form of intelligence,[2] many reporting that "they" wanted to teach them. One male subject said: "They were trying to show me as much as possible. They were communicating in words. They were like clowns or jokers or jesters or imps. There were just so many of them doing their funny little thing."[3]

Jester-like attire such as the multi-pointed hat worn by fairy, or dwarf-like beings has been found even in ancient Mayan art, as shown in Churchward's *The Sacred Symbols of Mu*.[4] Both the ancient Egyptians and the Central American peoples, right back to the Olmecs, had a special liking and reverence for dwarves. In both cases it was believed that dwarves were *directly connected to the gods*. And in both cases, dwarves were favoured as dancers and were shown as such in works of art.[5] It is interesting to note that some witnesses of fairies have seen them dancing in a circle (creating a vortex), mimicking the rotational motion associated with UFOs,[6] as if they used this method to create a dimensional portal as a UFO today might increase its frequency to shift between worlds/dimensions.

Ancient aboriginal rock art found in Western Australia in the 1800s clearly depicts a disc shaped UFO; smaller, spherical orbs much like those filmed so many times in recent history; a crop circle; a large cigar-like UFO; a spaceman; and what looks like a form of wave radiation emanating from the disc-shaped UFO. All of this is bordered and encompassed by a depiction of a snake; an ancient and global symbol of wisdom and knowledge, particularly for shamans in their spirit world journeys and for ancient cultures in general (for instance, the ancient Quiche Maya sacred book, the Popol Vu, features the plumed/feathered serpent, Quetzalcoatl,* the symbol of creation, which the Aztecs later morphed into the god of the same moniker[7]).

Within the serpentine border, in the bottom right corner, are two figures, one male and the other female according to Everard. Only their heads are depicted, but what is interesting is what Everard describes as their oddly "European" appearance, something the natives who created the art certainly did not possess. Everard points out that ancient Central and South American art also features these strangely "European" entities (note the previous Mayan example) despite there being no such people in these regions at the time. In these latter cultures they were referred to as the Viracocha; beings who came from the stars or from "across the seas" and gave the people knowledge of mathematics and astronomy, playing civilising roles. Everard notes the "female" figure's pointed hat as being akin to a "medieval jester's hat" which is, as he says, "very strange."[8]

Perhaps some of the "European" characters, Everard notes, are a different kind of being or phenomenon to the Viracochas, who history records as bearded demigods who cajoled man into civilisation as we know it. They have been credited with the creation of a great ancient Peruvian civilisation and the mysterious Nazca lines, massive ancient pictograms carved into the desert that can only be properly viewed aerially, among much else. The evidence suggests that the high god Viracocha had been worshipped by all the civilisations that had ever existed in the long history of Peru. The Incas had also built a temple to him at Cuzco.[9] Descriptions of Viracocha depict him as a typical Caucasian, somewhat similar in appearance to Jesus, though older. His behaviour was of the same mould as Jesus' also, though he possessed expertise in many fields, including science, healing, architecture, metallurgy, writing, and language.[10] (Rumour has it he could also touch his nose with his tongue.) Such miraculous wielding of healing abilities and technological wizardry as attributed to Viracocha, the "shining ones," are also regularly attributed to aliens and, in the past, to fairies and their equivalents—though fairies have, like "aliens," in many cases, been noted for their cruelty or hostility, unlike the Viracocha

* Among the Mexican and Central American Indians Quetzalcoatl was venerated as the incarnation of the spirit of the planet Venus. (Manly P. Hall, Reincarnation, The Philosophical Research Society, 1978, p 134.) Venus is the 'morning star' or 'light bringer,' so this is a curious link.

[1] G. Hancock, Supernatural, Disinformation Company Ltd, 2007, p 185-6. See also p 187 for another reference to jester-like attire.

[2] Strassman, DMT, Park Street Press, 2001, p 185.

[3] Ibid., p 192.

[4] Colonel James Churchward, The Sacred Symbols of Mu, B.E. Books/The C.W. Daniel Company Ltd., 1988, p 131, Figure A.

[5] Hancock, p 153.

[6] Ibid., pp 216-224.

[7] Churchward, pp 197-8

[8] Chris Everard, Secret Space 2, 2007 (film).

[9] Hancock, Fingerprints of the Gods, Three Rivers Press, 1995, p 46. See also Chapters 1-5.

[10] Ibid., pp 48-52.

SCIENCE & SPIRITUALITY

Brendan D. Murphy is a researcher, speaker, musician, and the author of The Grand Illusion: A Synthesis of Science and Spirituality – Book 1 (TGI 1), described by author Sol Luckman as a "masterpiece." Brendan is also a certified Psych-K facilitator, a certified DNA Potentiator (Potentiation is the first DNA activation in Luckman's Regenetics Method) and has received formal EFT training (levels 1 and 2). The Grand Illusion—along with free book excerpts and articles—is available at www.brendandmurphy.net. .

Nymph-ish Creations
Stone and clay creations for the Fae in us all

Necklaces, Wands, Jars, Smudge Sticks
www.facebook.com/NymphCreations

Artwork by **Nicolle**

www.facebook.com/ArtworkByNicolle
artworkbynicolle@bigpond.com

Muddy Hands and Feet - Balance with Faerie Magic

Rita Maher reminds us of connecting children to the simple joys of childhood past times that are oft forgotten in today's technological world, and the faeries will thank you for it too!

Muddy hands and feet, giggles and laughter resonate in the air, the days are long and the sun is warm, outdoor play for everyone. Dancing around the mushroom circles, sunlight glimmers on the morning dew, sprinkles of magic floating in the air. Foxgloves and Forget-Me-Nots sway gentle in the wind, while the fragrant jasmine fills the air. Magic is truly everywhere.

Summer could be filled with this wonderful whimsical magic where faery come and play, children allow their imagination to run wild as they build tiny faery houses and plant their favourite flowers. Creating magical doorways and leaving gifts of honey milk. Digging in the soil, squishing mud between their toes not caring how dirty they are, just enjoying life.

Or will summer be a battle of wills will it be a screaming match of get out the iPad, turn the computer off, leave the Xbox alone. Get outside get some fresh air? Sounds familiar I bet to just about any house with children in these days. Yes technology is a wonderful tool and the apps that they create are designed to mesmerise, entice and entrap the mind, just one more go, have another life. All of which brings the participant into a cocooned secluded world devoid of human and social interaction. Now please do not misunderstand me, I am well aware that there are some great games and apps that have been cleverly designed to teach children while entertaining them. Our children need to understand technology to survive in today's world. However there must be something said about the tipping of the scales that we have seen over the past few years. No longer do our children play in the streets; no longer do they relish the outdoors. More and more they are becoming solitary people whose idea of social interaction is a computer screen. So how do we swing the scales back so they are balanced when even the youngest of children these days are enticed to interact with computers and forget the outside world?

So what if I said take away the electronics for a day and head outside and create a magical environment for your child to nurture. Be it big or small there is surely a garden pot, wheel barrow or baron area of your garden that could use some TLC. Parents don't worry about the dirty clothes they can be washed, mud everywhere calls for a hosing down or water fight on a summer's day. When they find the worm and bring it to you don't squirm and shriek, instead explain the wonderful job they do for the earth. Take your child down to the local garden store and pick out some flowers or vegetables they would love to grow, grab some rocks, be creative with sticks and make a little house. Crystals can adorn the area, perhaps some wind chimes as well.

Let your child be in charge of planting and decorating this little creation of magic, get them to tend to it through the week, and on lazy summer afternoons even sit there and read them their favourite book. Playdates with friends can enjoy afternoon tea parties in the garden. Watch their eyes light up as they harvest vegetables and help you cook them that same day. All of this invites in the magic of the faeries, they love to be around those who care and nurture with a kind heart this earth. Faeries will help tend to the garden; they may even give glimpses of themselves to those around them with flashes of light.

By being outdoors and connecting back with nature makes a child's inner beauty glow, by being there with your child and sharing in this magic your inner beauty glows as well. Computer games can leave one irritated and frustrated, for children it can be hard to turn the mind off after playing them. Yet grounding, becoming calm and recharging ones energy is effortless when you head out doors and spend time in the garden. Bring balance back into life and enjoy the whimsical magic of the faeries who will delight in your child's connection with mother earth.

Rita Maher is a Psychic Medium, Intuitive Counsellor and qualified Reiki Healer who has a passion for working with children and families. She specialises in meditation and intuitive guidance to help not just children but adults understand direction and change in their life, helping create secure environments for young minds to grow and thrive.

Spirit Meals: Welcome Magic

Denise and Meadow Linn welcome the fae and all that is magical into their home with this delightful excerpt from their book 'The Mystic Cookbook', reprinted with permission from publisher Hay House…

It's possible to have a delightful, magical evening with your angel friends . . . real angels. It's true. You can indeed share a meal with angels, fairies, spirit guides, or possibly even a deceased loved one. The Spirit realm is simply a thought away, and it's completely possible to have spiritual beings join you around your dining table. These meals may be some of the most magical evenings you'll ever enjoy, and the Mystic Chef is always ready for celestial guests!

Invite the Fairy Folk for Dinner

The betwixt and between times have long been considered the domain of fairies, so you may wish to plan your fairy party for dusk or dawn. Create beautiful invitations that bring to mind times of enchantment. Don't forget to mail an invitation to the Fairy Folk, or simply put out the call by saying, "We invite you fairies, near and far, to share a meal with us."

As you would for any ceremony, prepare yourself and dress in clothing worthy of celebration. A leisurely salt bath is best, as the purity of the salt will align your energies to the otherworldliness of the fairy people. If unable to take a bath or shower, scrub yourself with a bit of sea salt.

As you decorate, incorporate natural, fairy-related items, such as acorns, bits of moss, crystals, flowers, or feathers. A valuable addition to any fairy meal is to spritz everything with carefully chosen flower essences. The highly calibrated vibration of flower essences will most certainly be inviting to those in the fairy realm. You may wish to have a bowl of fairy dust with a big brush in it for your guests to brush on themselves upon arrival. It has been said that primroses allow you to see the fairies, so some potted primroses may be appropriate.

The seat of honor belongs to the fairies, so make sure their glass is full and their plate is beautifully arranged. When planning the menu, choose foods that feel fun and spritely. Fairies frolic in nature and enjoy natural products, but they also enjoy honey, fruit, and other sweet treats. You may even wish to have this be a Fairy Nibbles party and serve little bites of everything. Think fresh berries, nuts and seeds, and petit fours. Of course, mead is traditional, but if there's no mead at your local wine store, substitute sparkling water, champagne, or elderflower liqueur.

After you've eaten and drunk and laughed and danced as the fairies would, thank them for honoring you with a visit to your home. Join hands and have each guest thank the fairies and share a few words or even a poem. The fairies do so love poetry!

To "see" Fairies in Nature:

- Eat lightly before you go out in nature—lettuce or raw vegetables is much better than fast food. If possible, nibble on edible flowers such as nasturtiums or rose petals.
- Drink natural spring water.
- Your clothes shouldn't be washed in perfumed detergent; natural unscented is best.
- Dab yourself with essential oils, and spritz yourself with flower essences. Rose is best, but flowers or plants from the area are excellent as well.
- Go outdoors someplace in nature or a park where you suspect fairies might reside.
- Mentally ask permission to enter. Approach slowly once you feel that permission has been granted.
- If there is anything in that area that is edible, put a tiny bit of it in your mouth, as this attunes you to the area. For example, put a tiny bit of rosemary, a wild blackberry, a rose petal, or a pine needle into your mouth.
- Sit still and allow your eyes to become non-focused, and be open to unusual movements of light or color. Chances are you've seen a fairy.

Meadow Linn is a writer and a chef, living in California with her dog, cats and chicken. She believes that living well and eating well should be tasty and fun. Meadow has just co-authored her first cookbook with Denise Linn which is available now through Amazon. **Contact Meadow at**: www.meadowlinn.com and www.savortheday.com

inSPIRIT | review

TAPPING THE WELL WITHIN

Published by Balboa Press
AUTHORED BY ALIX MOORE

Alix Moore has written a divinely inSpired book to help you unlock your creativity and allow the flow of inSpiration. Written for authors, this book and its step by step wisdom will benefit many other creative types as well.

From the simple daily practices of energy work and meditation, overcoming writer's block to the author sharing her personal insights and daily routines, this book will guide and support you to balance your creativity and the demands of everyday life. Alix's heartfelt wish to help and support you is felt throughout the pages of this book and as an author myself, I found myself eager to keep reading wondering what magic tip she would have that could assist me.

A must read for all aspiring authors or those seeking balance in life.

SEA SYMBOLS - JANARRIC RUNES

Spell Casting and Insight Card Deck
PUBLISHED AND AUTHORED BY GEM~MER - CRYSHELL MAGIC

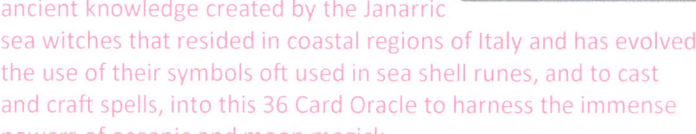

A truly unique offering in today's Oracle Card market, Gem~mer draws upon the ancient knowledge created by the Janarric sea witches that resided in coastal regions of Italy and has evolved the use of their symbols oft used in sea shell runes, and to cast and craft spells, into this 36 Card Oracle to harness the immense powers of oceanic and moon magick.

Easy to hold and simple to use, the cards can be used in four ways, to Spell Cast, for Daily Guidance, for Insight and Sea-Self Spread. Not only myself, but many I know who have used this deck have found it unerringly accurate with its messages offered for guidance seeked. The Guide Book offers clear and concise definitions for all of the Sea Symbols.

A wonderful addition to an experienced Oracle Card readers' collection and for novices alike.

inSPIRIT | Directory

ANIMAL SHAMANISM

BILLIE DEAN
Animal Shaman, Author, Teacher, Filmmaker
www.billiedean.com

AROMATHERAPY

THE SCENTED LOTUS
Aromatherapy Oils & Blends
www.thescentedlotus.com
E: thescentedlotus@hotmail.com

ARTWORK

NICOLLE POLL
Artwork by Nicolle - Oracle Cards, Animal Magick Series, Soul Journey Portraits
E: artworkbynicolle@bigpond.com
FB: www.facebook.com/ArtworkByNicolle

NICOLA MCINTOSH
Graphic Design, Fairy & Fantasy Art, Oracle Cards & Writer
www.nicolamcintosh.com

ASSOCIATIONS

www.ciema.org

ASTROLOGERS

DAVID WELLS
Teacher, Qabalist, Astrologer, Author & Past Life Therapist
www.davidwells.co.uk

CRYSTAL SHOPS

JOPO FENG SHUI & CRYSTALS
2 Revesby Road, Revesby NSW
T: +612 9785 0798

SPIRIT STONE
For crystals & new age supplies
www.spiritstone.com.au

MAGICAL TOOLS

NATASHA HEARD
Blessed Branches
www.blessedbranches.com

GEM~MER
Cryshell Magic
www.cryshellmagic.com.au

PAST LIVES

SACRED FAMILIAR
Julia Inglis & Tony Esta
Author, Past Life Healings & Workshops
www.sacredfamiliar.com

PERSONAL GROWTH

KYE CROW
Wunjo Crow – Sacred Clothing, Animal Sanctuary & Sacred Journey into the Animal Realm workshops
www.camelcampsanctuary.com
www.facebook.com/Wunjocrow

Would you like your listing included here? Email us at
mail@inspiritpublishing.net for details.

PSYCHICS & MEDIUMS

KERRIE WEARING
Author, Soul Coach & Medium
www.psychicmedium.com.au

SCIENCE & SPIRITUALITY

BRENDAN D. MURPHY
Author - The Grand Illusion
www.brendandmurphy.net

SHAMANISM

LAURA NAOMI
Consultations, Workshops & Seminars
www.globaldreamwhisperer.com

STORYTELLING & FOLKLORE

REILLY McCARRON
Faerie Bard, Folklorist & Storyteller with Harp
www.faeriebard.com
E: info@faeriebard.com
F: Faerie Bard

RADIO SHOWS

www.ghostsofoz.com

Kerrie Wearing
Author ~ Soul Coach ~ Medium ~ Publisher

Join my Soul inSpired Living community today and as my gift to you, receive a FREE copy of my ebook *Your Soul Self, Experience the Soul through Past Life Recognition.*

Its full of wisdom, inSights, meditations and exercises to strengthen your Soul connection.

JOIN NOW. ITS FREE!

www.psychicmedium.com.au

Summer / December 2013
The Faery Issue
www.inspiritmagazine.com

www.ingramcontent.com/pod-product-compliance
Lightning Source LLC
Chambersburg PA
CBHW041120300426
44112CB00002B/40